Fact Finders™

Energy at Work

Nuclear Power

by Josepha Sherman

Consultant:
Steve Brick, Associate Director
Energy Center of Wisconsin
Madison, Wisconsin

Capstone press
Mankato, Minnesota

−241 3921

Fact Finders is published by Capstone Press,
151 Good Counsel Drive, P.O. Box 669, Mankato, Minnesota 56002.
www.capstonepress.com

Library of Congress Cataloging-in-Publication Data
Sherman, Josepha.
    Nuclear power / by Josepha Sherman.
    p. cm.—(Fact finders. Energy at work)
    Summary: Introduces the history, uses, production, advantages and disadvantages,
and future of nuclear energy as a power resource.
    Includes bibliographical references and index.
    ISBN 0-7368-2473-1 (hardcover)
    ISBN 0-7368-5193-3 (paperback)
    1. Nuclear engineering—Juvenile literature. 2. Nuclear power plants—Juvenile
literature. [1. Nuclear energy.] I. Title. II. Series.
TK9148.S34 2004
333.792'4—dc22   2003015052

Editorial Credits

Gillia Olson, editor; Juliette Peters, designer; Alta Schaffer, photo researcher; Eric Kudalis,
    product planning editor

Photo Credits

Cover: Nogent Nuclear Power Station in France, Corbis/Julia Waterlow; Eye Ubiquitous

Corbis, 10–11; Corbis/Charles E. Rotkin, 12; Charles O'Rear, 25; Martin Marietta/
    Roger Ressmeyer, 8; Roger Ressmeyer, 21, 24; Royalty Free, 1, 7; Tim Wright, 18
Corbis Sygma/Kostin Igor, 14; Robert Patrick, 13
Getty Images Inc./Robert Laberga, 22–23; Sean Gallup, 15; SPL, 4–5
Index Stock Imagery/Gary Conner, 27; Hoa Qui, 16–17
Photri-Microstock, 19

1 2 3 4 5 6 09 08 07 06 05 04

Table of Contents

Chapter 1

Chain Reaction

In Chicago in 1942, scientists gathered in front of a clicking clocklike dial. Behind that, draped in gray cloth, sat a pile of gray metal bricks. The scientists liked to call it "the Pile."

Inside the Pile, unseen and unheard, tiny particles banged into each other. They hit so hard that they sometimes split in two. The dial clicked along with these hits, measuring them.

George Weil held onto a rod sticking out from the Pile. The rod kept too many particles from crashing. Then Weil pulled out the rod a little. The clicking turned into a steady hum. The hits were increasing.

George Weil pushed and pulled a rod in and out of the Pile as scientists measured the number of crashing particles.

After 28 minutes, Weil pushed the rod back into the Pile. The clicking stopped. The scientists smiled and clapped. They had just witnessed the first controlled nuclear **chain reaction**.

Chapter 2

Splitting Atoms

Long ago, the Greeks believed that everything was made of four elements. The elements were fire, air, earth, and water. Greek philosopher Democritus said that the elements were made up of tiny pieces called **atoms**. Democritus believed that nothing was smaller than an atom.

Today, we know that an atom is an element in its smallest form. But atoms are made up of even smaller pieces. Every atom is made up of **protons**, **neutrons**, and **electrons**. The **nucleus** is the center of an atom. The nucleus is made up of protons and neutrons. Electrons travel around the nucleus.

proton

nucleus

neutron

electron

Ancient Greeks thought fire, air, earth, and water were the only four elements.

Inset: An atom contains a nucleus of protons and neutrons. Electrons travel around the nucleus.

▲ Uranium is a heavy,
silvery metal.

FACT!

Uranium is very heavy.
A gallon of milk weighs
8 pounds (3.6 kilograms),
but a piece of uranium
the same size weighs
150 pounds (68 kilograms).

Fission

Nuclear energy comes from changes in the center of an atom. Some atoms can split in two. This splitting is called **nuclear fission**. When an atom splits, it gives off heat. This heat can be used to make electricity.

Uranium is the most common element used in nuclear power plants. It is a silvery metal. When a uranium atom splits, a few neutrons are released. These neutrons crash into other uranium atoms, splitting them. This process continues and becomes a chain reaction.

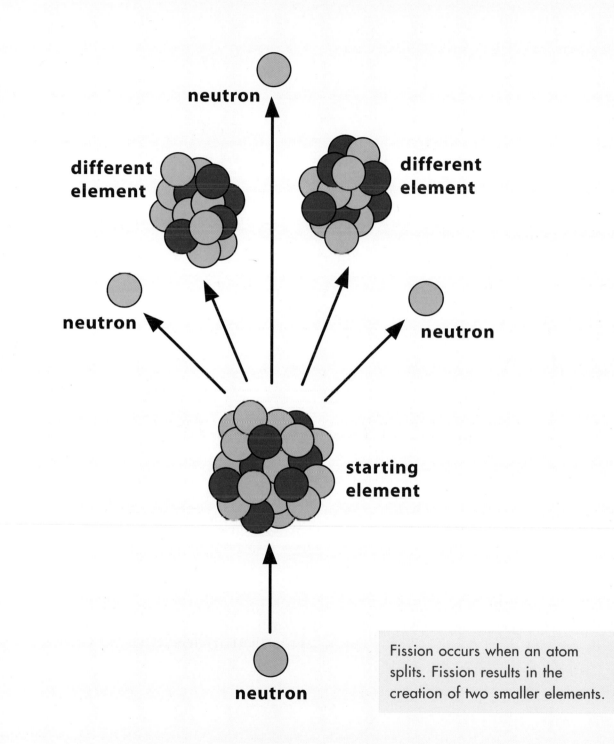

neutron

different
element

neutron

different
element

neutron

starting
element

neutron

Fission occurs when an atom splits. Fission results in the creation of two smaller elements.

Chapter 3

Nuclear History

People knew about atoms for thousands of years. They did not know atoms could be used to create energy until the 1900s.

Fission and the Bomb

The work of several scientists led to the discovery of fission. In 1934, Italian scientist Enrico Fermi was the first person to split a uranium atom. In 1938, Germans Otto Hahn and Fritz Strassman also split an atom of uranium. Their experiments showed that fission creates large amounts of energy.

The atomic bomb dropped on Nagasaki in 1945 showed the power of nuclear energy.

People first used fission for atomic weapons. During World War II (1939–1945), the United States built atomic bombs. In 1945, the first atomic bombs were dropped on Hiroshima and Nagasaki in Japan. At least 110,000 people were killed instantly.

Electricity from Nuclear Power

After the war, scientists wanted to find a way to use fission to make electricity. In 1956, the world's first nuclear power plant was built in England. Nuclear power plants were soon built in many other countries. In 1957, the first U.S. nuclear plant opened in Shippingport, Pennsylvania.

Calder Hall, the first nuclear power plant, was built in England.

Radiation

Uranium gives off unseen particles called **radiation**. Nuclear reactions also give off radiation. Some of this radiation can sicken or kill people, animals, and plants. Radiation poisoning killed 250,000 people in Japan after the atomic bombings of World War II.

Safety has always been an issue with nuclear power. A nuclear power plant will not blow up like a bomb, but it can leak radiation.

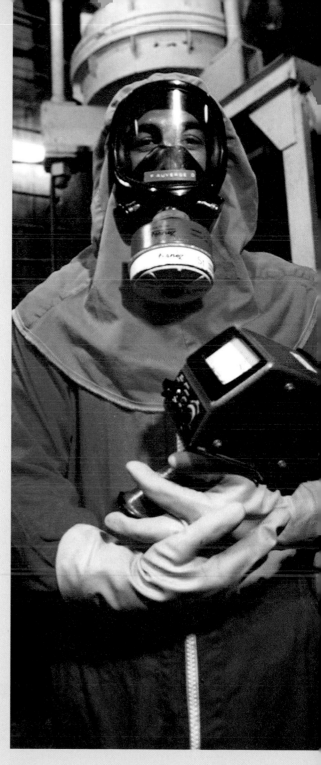

Workers wear suits to protect themselves from most radiation.

▲ Workers clean up the area after the Chernobyl disaster. Many workers later died of radiation poisoning.

Accidents

In 1979, an accident occurred at the Three Mile Island Nuclear Power Plant in Pennsylvania. The plant was badly damaged. Only a little radiation escaped.

In 1986, the Chernobyl Power Plant in the Ukraine had a serious accident. A large amount of radiation was released. Nearly 100 people later died from radiation poisoning.

Since then, most nuclear power plants have operated very safely. Nuclear energy remains a dependable, cheap power source. At the end of 2002, 441 nuclear power plants were operating around the world.

This plant in the Czech Republic is just one of 441 nuclear plants ▼ around the world.

Chapter 4

Creating Electricity

Nuclear power plants create reactions in buildings called nuclear reactors. The nuclear reaction happens in the center of the reactor, called the reactor core.

Uranium

Power plants must get uranium to use in their reactors. Uranium is found in rocks in the earth. People mine and prepare uranium. The uranium is then made into small pellets about the size of baby carrots.

The reactor core is filled with water when it is in operation.

Fuel and Control Rods

Uranium pellets are put in metal tubes called fuel rods. The rods are about 11.5 feet (3.5 meters) long. Large plants can have up to 75,000 fuel rods in a reactor.

Control rods are put in among the fuel rods. Control rods are made out of elements that soak up neutrons. Workers control machines that push in or pull out control rods. Pulling out a control rod starts the reaction. Pushing in a rod slows down or stops the nuclear reaction.

A used fuel rod is pulled out of a reactor. The spent rods glow.

▲ Control rods
usually come
in from the top
of a reactor.

After fuel rods and control
rods are in place, a nuclear
reactor is filled with a moderator.
Water is the most common
moderator. The moderator slows
down the neutrons. Slower
neutrons are more likely to hit
another atom, keeping the chain
reaction going.

Making Electricity

Nuclear power plants heat water in the core with energy from fission. The water is then piped through a tank of water. This water boils to make steam.

The steam turns turbines. These fan-shaped machines are connected to a generator. The generator makes electricity. The steam is then cooled. It is sent back through the system to be used again.

Nuclear plants keep the core water separate from the rest of the system to keep radiation contained.

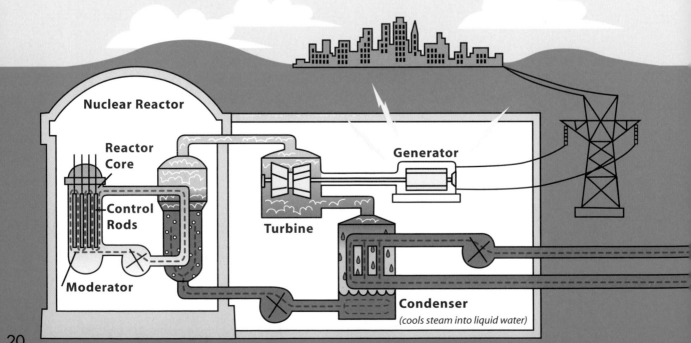

Nuclear Reactor

Reactor Core

Control Rods

Moderator

Turbine

Generator

Condenser
(cools steam into liquid water)

Radiation and Waste

Nuclear power plants are heavily shielded to stop radiation from leaking out. The reactor is surrounded by 3 feet (1 meter) of concrete and steel.

When uranium no longer makes enough energy, it must be stored correctly. Nuclear waste gives off strong radiation. The waste must be covered until it no longer can harm people. It is stored in pools of water at the plant for about 40 years. In some countries, the waste is then buried in containers deep underground. The United States has no such storage areas at this time.

Spent fuel rods are stored in pools of water for 40 years or more.

Chapter 5

Benefits and Drawbacks

About 17 percent of the world's energy comes from nuclear power. Like all other energy sources, nuclear energy has benefits and drawbacks.

Benefits

Nuclear power does not dirty the air when it is made. Fossil fuels, such as oil and coal, are burned to make electricity. Their smoke pollutes the air.

Small amounts of uranium can make large amounts of energy. A handful of uranium can make as much electricity as seven train cars loaded with coal.

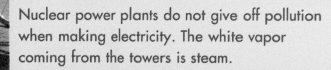

Nuclear power plants do not give off pollution
when making electricity. The white vapor
coming from the towers is steam.

Drawbacks

Nuclear waste gives off dangerous radiation for more than 1,000 years. Safely storing this waste is a problem. The waste must be covered to stop radiation leaks. It also must be stored in a safe place without being bothered. It is hard to be sure that people can keep nuclear waste safely stored for more than 1,000 years.

Workers often check radiation levels at waste ▼ storage sites.

▲ This breeder
nuclear reactor
recycles uranium.

FACT!

All of the nuclear waste
made in the United
States over the last
40 years would cover a
football field 15 feet
(4.6 meters) deep.

Like coal and oil,
uranium is a nonrenewable
resource. It will eventually
run out. Scientists are trying
to make the most of the
limited amount of uranium
on Earth. They have found
ways to recycle uranium.
The uranium can then be
used again.

Chapter 6

Is Fusion the Future?

Scientists are trying to use a type of nuclear energy called **nuclear fusion**. The Sun gets its energy this way. In nuclear fusion, the nuclei of two atoms join to make another element.

Fusion makes a lot of energy. It also creates very little waste. The atoms used come from common elements like hydrogen.

Currently, fusion costs too much to use. The fuel, process, and machinery are expensive. Scientists are trying to find ways to make fusion cheaper.

A worker adjusts an experimental fusion machine.

Nuclear power will continue to be an important energy source. It is dependable, clean, and safe. For a long-term future, people need to find a safe way to store nuclear waste.

Fast Facts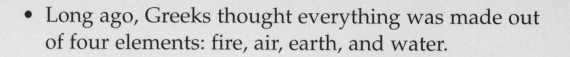

- Long ago, Greeks thought everything was made out of four elements: fire, air, earth, and water.

- The atom is the smallest form of an element. It is made up of protons, neutrons, and electrons.

- During nuclear fission, a neutron hits the nucleus of another atom and splits it.

- Uranium gives off unseen particles called radiation. Some radiation can sicken or kill living things.

- Nuclear waste must be covered until it can no longer harm people. It must be covered for 1,000 years or more.

- Nuclear energy is a nonrenewable resource.

- Nuclear energy is clean and cheap to make, but waste disposal makes people worry about this energy.

Hands On: Chain Reaction

What You Need

at least 15 dominoes and a level surface

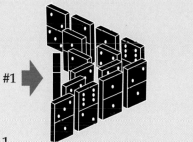

diagram 1

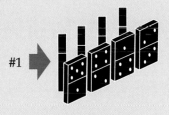

diagram 2

What You Do

1. Place the dominoes as shown in diagram 1. Hit domino #1. The dominoes show an uncontrolled reaction. All of the neutrons released when a uranium atom splits are allowed to hit other atoms. This action releases even more neutrons. Nuclear bombs use these types of reactions to create explosions.

2. Place the dominoes as shown in diagram 2. Hit domino #1. The dominoes show a controlled reaction. Only one neutron is allowed to continue the chain reaction, making a steady rate of energy. This type of reaction is used to make electricity in nuclear power plants.

Glossary

atom (AT-uhm)—an element in its smallest form

chain reaction (CHAYN ree-AK-shuhn)—a series of reactions that cause more reactions of the same kind

electron (ee-LEK-tron)—a tiny particle in an atom that travels around the nucleus

neutron (NOO-trahn)—one of the very small parts in an atom's nucleus; when neutrons hit some atoms, the atoms will split.

nuclear fission (NYOO-klee-ur FISH-uhn)—the splitting of the nucleus of an atom, which creates energy

nuclear fusion (NYOO-klee-ur FYOO-shuhn)—the joining of two nuclei, which creates energy

nucleus (NYOO-klee-uhss)—the center of an atom; a nucleus is made up of neutrons and protons; two or more are called nuclei.

proton (PRO-tahn)—one of the very small parts in an atom's nucleus

radiation (ray-dee-AY-shuhn)—tiny particles sent out from radioactive material

Internet Sites

FactHound offers a safe, fun way to find Internet sites related to this book. All of the sites on FactHound have been researched by our staff.

Here's how:

1. Visit *www.facthound.com*
2. Type in this special code **0736824731** for age-appropriate sites. Or enter a search word related to this book for a more general search.
3. Click on the Fetch It button.

FactHound will fetch the best sites for you!

Read More

Graham, Ian S. *Nuclear Power.* Energy Forever. Austin, Texas: Raintree Steck-Vaughn, 1999.

Morgan, Nina. *Nuclear Power.* Twentieth Century Inventions. Austin, Texas: Raintree Steck-Vaughn, 1998.

Richardson, Hazel. *How to Split the Atom.* New York: Franklin Watts, 2001.

Snedden, Robert. *Nuclear Energy.* Essential Energy. Chicago: Heinemann Library, 2002.

Index